My Own Sacred Grove

For Carter, Janey, and McKay,
the reasons I write.
And for my husband, Derek,
who makes it all possible.
–Angie

For Micah, Naomi, Adam, and Lincoln,
the heroes who delight and inspire me every day.
–Alyssa

ISBN 13: 978-1-4621-4332-0

Published by CFI, an imprint of Cedar Fort, Inc.
2373 W. 700 S., Suite 100, Springville, UT 84663
Distributed by Cedar Fort, Inc., www.cedarfort.com

Library of Congress Control Number: 2022941444

Cover design and interior layout by Shawnda T. Craig

Printed in the United States of America

10 9 8 7 6 5 4 3 2 1

Printed on acid-free paper

My Own Sacred Grove

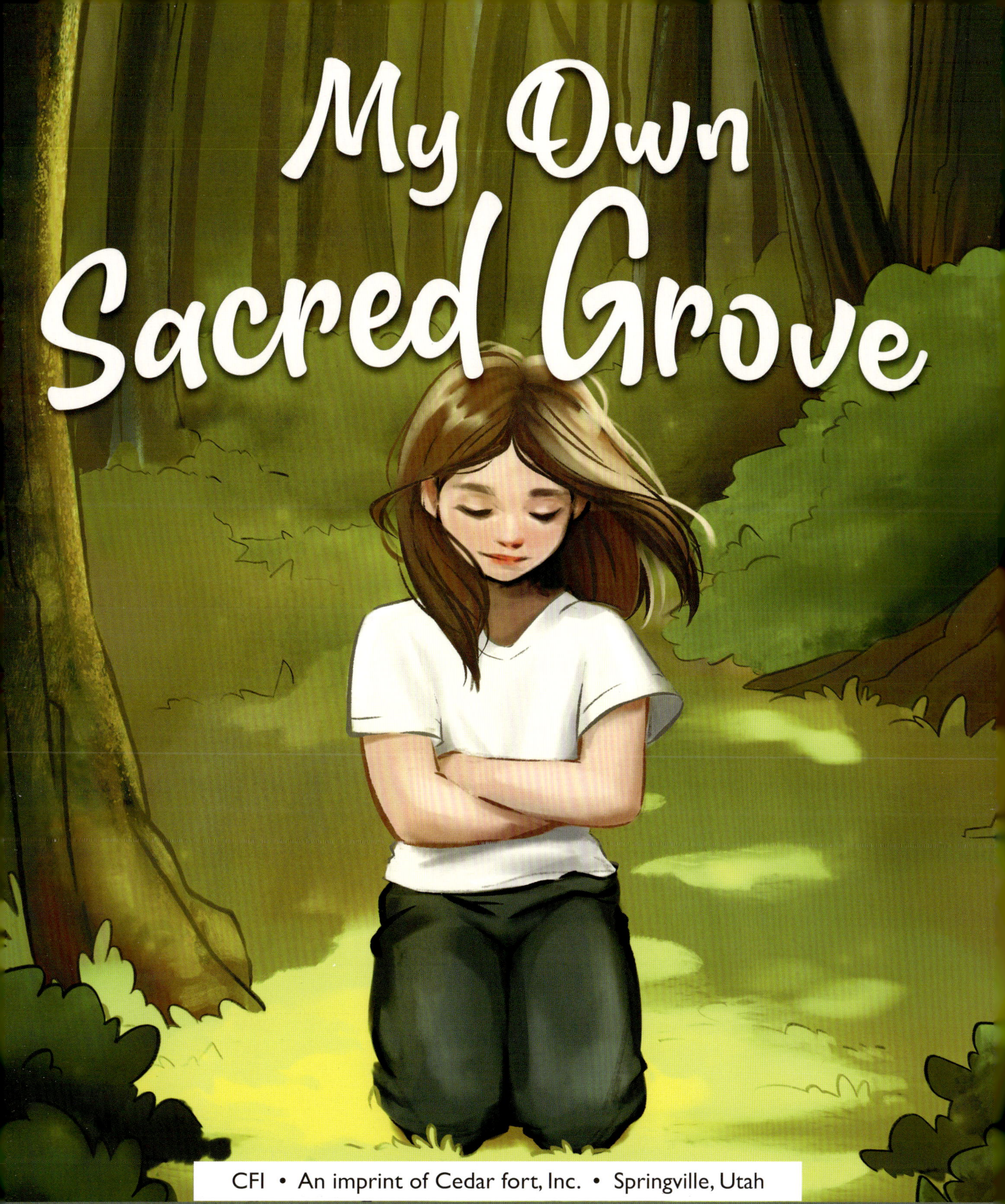

CFI • An imprint of Cedar fort, Inc. • Springville, Utah

written by Angie Killian • illustrations by Alyssa Harper

Joseph Smith went
to a grove full of trees.

Seeking God's wisdom,

he fell to his knees.

As he pled with
the heavens, the sky
filled with light,

and the Father appeared
with His Son, Jesus Christ,

standing above in the air,

coming to answer his prayer.

I will find my own sacred grove
away from all of the noise of the world.

I will turn to prayer,
for I know He's there.
I will find my own
sacred grove.

So many choices
with so much at stake.
Life's full of pathways,
but which should I take?

If I lift up in prayer
in the name of the Son,
through the power of the
Holy Ghost, answers will come.

Heavenly Father is there,

ready to answer my prayer.

I will find my own sacred grove
away from all of the noise of the world.
I will turn to prayer, for I know He's there.
I will find my own sacred grove.

Sometimes the
answers take time,

so I'll listen in
heart and mind.

Revelation will come my way

as I wait patiently in faith.

I will find my own sacred grove
away from all of the noise of the world.
I will turn to prayer, for I know He's there.
I will find my own sacred grove.

I will find my own sacred grove.